How to

C000173588

BOWLS

a step·by·step guide

Series editor:
Mike Shaw

Technical consultants:
John Fox, Former Secretary,
Norfolk District of the
English Bowling Association

R. Holt, Secretary, British
Crown Green Bowling Association

JARROLD

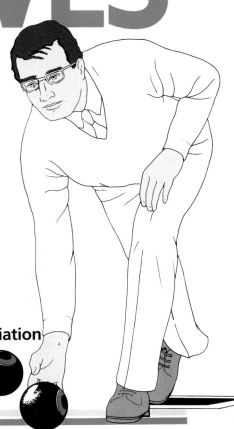

Other titles in this series are:

AMERICAN FOOTBALL	**SAILING A DINGHY**
BADMINTON	**SNOOKER**
BASKETBALL	**SOCCER**
COARSE FISHING	**SQUASH**
CRICKET	**SWIMMING**
CROQUET	**TABLE TENNIS**
GET FIT FOR SPORT	**TENNIS**
GOLF	**TABLE TENNIS**
HOCKEY	**WINDSURFING**

How to play BOWLS
ISBN 0-7117-0424-2

Text © Mike Shaw 1989
This edition © Jarrold Publishing 1989
Illustrations by Malcolm Ryan

First published 1989
Reprinted 1996

Designed and produced by
Parke Sutton Limited, Norwich
for Jarrold Publishing, Norwich
Printed in Great Britain. 2/96

Contents

Introduction

Bowls perhaps has the reputation of being an older person's game but television coverage and the fairly recent rapid expansion of indoor bowls has done much to dispel that image.

Bowls is a game for both men and women of any age and any level of skill. The indoor rink has made it an all-year game and it is not expensive to take up as most municipal parks and indoor rinks hire out bowls. It is also a pleasantly sociable game of skill and infinite variety. No end of bowls is ever the same.

Unlike many games, bowls can be played by a large or small group — from just two players up to forty or more playing adjacent to each other. The nature of bowls also allows players of differing standards to play together. In the game of fours, for example, an inexperienced player would play first leaving the tactics and complicated shots to more experienced colleagues. None the less, what better way to learn?

Two types of bowls games are covered in this book:- Flat Green (on pages 6 - 36) and Crown Green (on pages 37 - 48).

Flat Green is the more traditional game played on a large green divided into several rinks. These can be found in municipal parks, some pubs, and at bowls clubs. There are also many fine full-size indoor rinks.

Crown Green is a game with northern roots played on a green with a raised area in the centre (hence the name). Although there are many similarities, the sloping surface makes for a very different technique.

In recent years another form of indoor bowls has been introduced and is becoming increasingly popular. Called 'Short Mat' bowls, it is a development of carpet bowls which uses full size bowls on a carpet six feet wide by forty-five feet long. A wooden block (called the centre bock or windmill) is positioned halfway up the rink to discourage firing. The rules and techniques of the Short Mat game are not covered in this book.

Whichever type of bowls is played it will be found to be a satisfying, not too energetic game, suitable for all ages.

The Green

The green is traditionally of grass, although the more recent indoor game is played on a variety of artificial surfaces. The rules state that the surface shall be level and surrounded by a ditch and a bank – forming the boundaries.

Greens should be square, not less than 120ft (114ft in indoor bowls) nor more than 132ft. However, some National Associations may allow greens with a minimum of 99ft in the direction of play. Provided greens are within these dimensions, however, they may also be rectangular.

The green is divided into rinks so several games can be played on a green simultaneously. The width of a rink should not be less than 16ft (14ft in domestic games, 15ft in indoor games) nor more than 19ft, so a maximum sized outdoor green could contain up to eight rinks.

The ditch and the bank are an essential part of the game. The ditch is between eight and fifteen inches wide, and between two and eight inches deep.

The bank must rise at least nine inches above the level of the green, and be vertical or at least lean outwards by no greater angle than 35°. White wooden pegs are fixed in the bank and green thread sometimes stretched tightly between them to mark the rinks, but for indoors the thread is usually kept in the side ditch and only taken to a rink to determine whether a bowl or Jack is in or out of that rink.

There is usually a marker on the bank to show players the exact centre of the rink. White pegs are fixed on the side bank to indicate a distance of 76ft from the end ditch (81ft indoors).

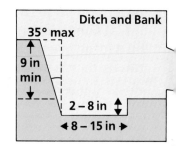

Ditch and Bank

35° max

9 in min

2 – 8 in

8 – 15 in

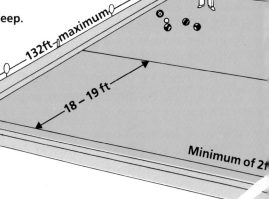

132ft maximum

18 – 19 ft

Minimum of 2ft

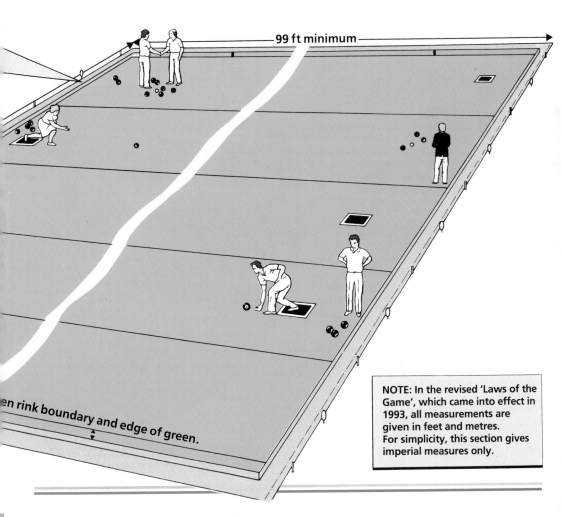

99 ft minimum

en rink boundary and edge of green.

NOTE: In the revised 'Laws of the Game', which came into effect in 1993, all measurements are given in feet and metres. For simplicity, this section gives imperial measures only.

Equipment

The bowls

Traditionally bowls were made of a dense South American hardwood called lignum vitae, but nowadays composition bowls are more popular. This is because wooden bowls can crack, lose weight, change bias and need more care. They are, however, more responsive in play and less affected by heavy greens. Bowls are still often referred to as 'woods'.

It is generally considered an advantage to play with a heavy bowl. The weight of a bowl is limited by its size, and the size of the bowl that can be played with is limited by the size of the hand of the player. Composition bowls are size for size heavier than lignum vitae bowls. If you take wooden and composition bowls of the same weight, the composition bowl will be roughly ⅛in. less in diameter.

Irrespective of size, the maximum weight of a bowl is 3½lbs. The minimum, for the smallest bowl, is approximately 2¾lbs. The maximum diameter of wooden bowls is 5¼in., and of composition bowls 5⅛in.

Bowls should be a matched set of four, of the same size and colour and each bearing the same unique identifying number and registered stamp of either the W B B (World Bowls Board) or the I B B (International Bowling Board) or the B I B B (British Isles Bowling Board). If of wood, they will have been made from the same log.

Bowls also have varying degrees of bias (see page 12), because the running surface of the bowl is slightly off-centre.

As a set of new bowls is expensive, it is a good idea to start with a good secondhand set.

When buying a secondhand set, make sure that they area a set, i.e. check that the size, serial number and any engraved design are identical (all this information is stamped on the bowl). Each bowl should also bear a legible registered I B B or B I B C stamp, preferably 1985 or later.

Bowls Size	0	01	1	2	3	4	5	6	7
Diameter (in.)	4⁹/₁₆	4¹¹/₁₆	4¾	4¹³/₁₆	4⅞	4¹⁵/₁₆	5	5¹/₁₆	5⅛

The mat

The mat is part of the game. It is rectangular, usually of rubber, measuring 24 x 14 inches. Most mats have a two-inch white border, but this is not obligatory.

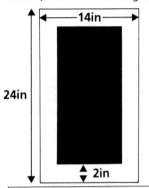

The Jack

The Jack is white and about 2½ inches in diameter (not less than $2^{15}/_{32}$ or more than $2^{17}/_{32}$, or $2^{21}/_{32}$ in indoor bowls). It can weigh between 8 and 10oz. In indoor bowls the Jack is much heavier – between 13½ and 16oz. It does not have a bias.

Ideal bowls size

A rule of thumb for your ideal bowl-size – select a bowl equal in circumference to a circle made by your thumbs and middle fingers. Alternatively, hold the bowl at arms length and turn your hand over so that the bowl is facing the ground. If the bowl tends to slip, it is too large.

Clothing

Dress

Traditionally white is worn by both men and women. Men wear ties.

The general rule in club play is white above the waist, grey below. These rules, however, only really apply to match play at a high level. Clubs have different rules governing, for example, the length of skirts, and it is best to ask the club captain what the form is.

Footwear

The condition of a bowling green is so crucial to the game that the rules stipulate that smooth-soled heel-less footwear must be worn at all times on the green.

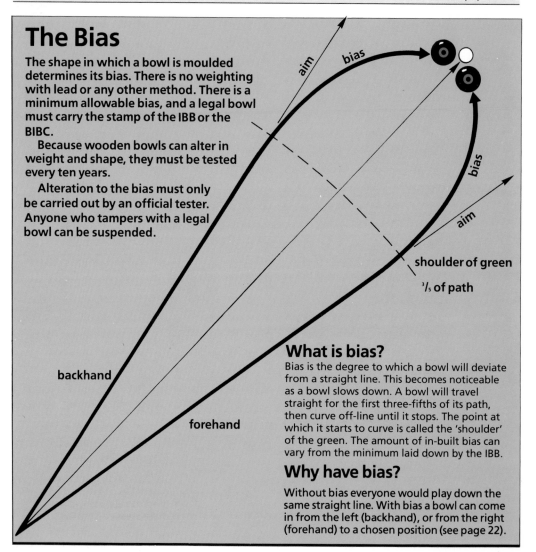

The Bias

The shape in which a bowl is moulded determines its bias. There is no weighting with lead or any other method. There is a minimum allowable bias, and a legal bowl must carry the stamp of the IBB or the BIBC.

Because wooden bowls can alter in weight and shape, they must be tested every ten years.

Alteration to the bias must only be carried out by an official tester. Anyone who tampers with a legal bowl can be suspended.

aim

bias

bias

aim

shoulder of green

³/₅ of path

backhand

forehand

What is bias?

Bias is the degree to which a bowl will deviate from a straight line. This becomes noticeable as a bowl slows down. A bowl will travel straight for the first three-fifths of its path, then curve off-line until it stops. The point at which it starts to curve is called the 'shoulder' of the green. The amount of in-built bias can vary from the minimum laid down by the IBB.

Why have bias?

Without bias everyone would play down the same straight line. With bias a bowl can come in from the left (backhand), or from the right (forehand) to a chosen position (see page 22).

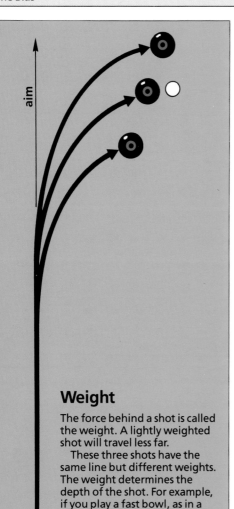

Weight

The force behind a shot is called the weight. A lightly weighted shot will travel less far.

These three shots have the same line but different weights. The weight determines the depth of the shot. For example, if you play a fast bowl, as in a firing shot, you will need to allow for very little bias.

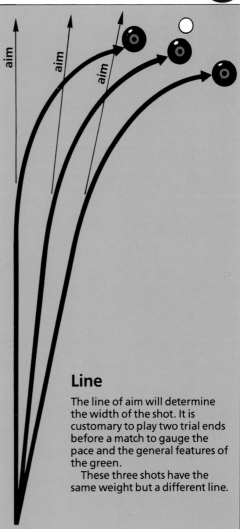

Line

The line of aim will determine the width of the shot. It is customary to play two trial ends before a match to gauge the pace and the general features of the green.

These three shots have the same weight but a different line.

The Mat

In the first end the front of the mat is positioned in the centre of the rink, exactly six feet from the back ditch. It stays in this position throughout the end.

At the beginning of subsequent ends the first player may choose to play long or short, as desired.

The longest play is with the front of the mat six feet from the back ditch; the shortest play with the front of the mat 76ft (indoors 81ft) from the front ditch.

The first player may position the mat anywhere between these two points and the mat remains in that position throughout the end.

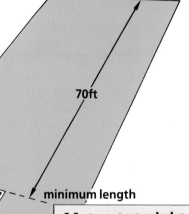

front ditch

70ft

minimum length

front of mat

6ft

back ditch

first end position and maximum length

Mat not straight

The mat must be straight and in the centre of the rink. If it gets out of alignment it may be straightened.

Mat moves

If the mat moves during play it must be repositioned as close as possible to the original position.

Delivering the Jack

An end starts with the delivery of the Jack by the first player. The Jack has no bias, so it rolls straight. The first player must roll the Jack so that it travels in a straight line at least 70ft (75ft indoors) from the front of the mat. The Jack is always moved to the centre of the rink (the 'centre line') after it has come to rest. This is called centering the Jack. If it travels less than 70ft, or goes out of the rink, or into the ditch, or if the player commits a foot fault (see page 23), it is redelivered by the other player. The Jack must be repositioned if it comes to rest closer to the front ditch than six feet.

Too close to ditch

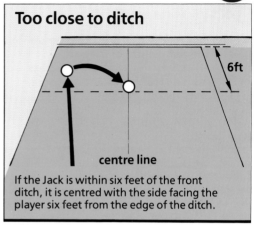

If the Jack is within six feet of the front ditch, it is centred with the side facing the player six feet from the edge of the ditch.

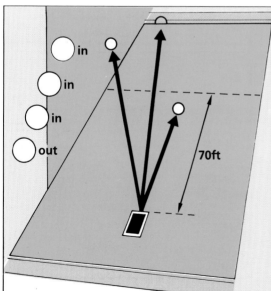

Redelivery

If the Jack does not travel 70ft (75ft indoors) or goes out, or goes into the ditch, the opposing lead delivers the Jack and may also reposition the mat if desired. He may not play the first bowl however – that remains the right of the first player. Close decisions may be queried and properly measured, but not once the first bowl has been delivered.

Should the Jack not travel 70ft, or go out or into the ditch on the second attempt, then the first player delivers the Jack and chooses the mat position.

If after four attempts the Jack has still not been properly delivered, it is repositioned centrally six feet from the front ditch and the position of the mat is chosen by the first player (except in the indoor game when the mat is placed on the centre line with its front edge left from the rear ditch).

Dead Bowls

A bowl may hit the Jack and other bowls, but for a bowl to count in the scoring it must be 'live' at the completion of the end.

A BOWL IS DEAD IF:

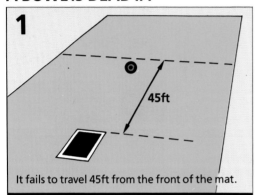

1

45ft

It fails to travel 45ft from the front of the mat.

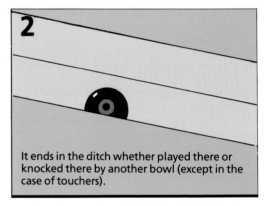

2

It ends in the ditch whether played there or knocked there by another bowl (except in the case of touchers).

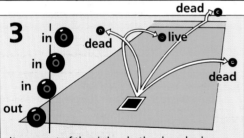

3

dead

in   dead   live

in

in

out   dead

It goes out of the rink, whether knocked or played. That is – the whole bowl ends up completely over either side line, or beyond the ditch and over the bank (there are no exceptions).

A bowl may leave the rink, be carried back in by the bias, and remain live.

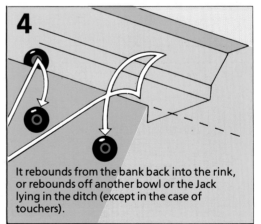

4

It rebounds from the bank back into the rink, or rebounds off another bowl or the Jack lying in the ditch (except in the case of touchers).

NOTE: A dead bowl is removed from the rink and placed on the bank at once.

Touchers

If on its original course a bowl touches the Jack it becomes a 'toucher'. Several privileges may be involved:

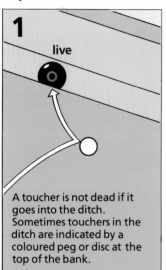

1

live

A toucher is not dead if it goes into the ditch. Sometimes touchers in the ditch are indicated by a coloured peg or disc at the top of the bank.

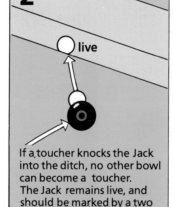

2

live

If a toucher knocks the Jack into the ditch, no other bowl can become a toucher. The Jack remains live, and should be marked by a two inch white peg on the top of the bank.

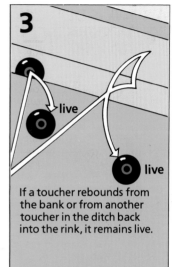

3

live

live

If a toucher rebounds from the bank or from another toucher in the ditch back into the rink, it remains live.

Dead touchers

Touchers, whether played or knocked out of the rink, become dead, and are removed at once onto the bank.

Marking touchers

Touchers are marked with chalk. If a toucher is not marked before the next bowl comes to rest, it ceases to be a toucher. If marking a bowl would disturb it a player may nominate it verbally instead. After an end, chalked bowls must be cleaned. If a bowl topples over after coming to rest and touches the Jack, it becomes a toucher providing:

1 The next bowl has not been delivered.

2 It is the last bowl and comes to rest within 30 seconds of the completion of the end.

Interruptions

There are several events which, although uncommon, do occur and require clarification. Remember – a live bowl cannot interrupt play. If it displaces another bowl or the Jack, it is a consequence of the game.

1 Non-toucher rebound

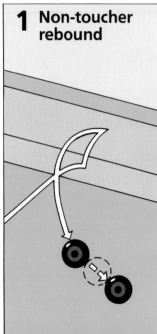

If a non-toucher rebounds from the bank and hits a live bowl or the Jack, the non-toucher, being dead, is removed and the live bowl or Jack is repositioned as near as possible to its original location by a player of the other side.

2 A player interrupts play

Should a player touch a bowl that is in motion – a live bowl, a toucher in the ditch, or the Jack – the opponent has four choices:

1 Reposition the bowl or Jack as near as possible to its original location.

2 Leave it where it is.

3 Declare the bowl or Jack dead. If the Jack is dead, however, the end is also dead.

4 Declare the end dead. The end is then re-played from the same direction, with the first player as before.

3 A non-player interrupts play

Should a spectator, a player from another rink, a foreign object, or a bowl from the next rink touch either a bowl in motion, a live bowl, a toucher in the ditch, or the Jack, then the players have three choices:

1 Agree on the repositioning of the affected bowl or Jack.

2 Declare the end dead and replay from the same direction, the first player as before.

3 If a bowl is displaced on its original course within the boundaries of the rink without having disturbed the head, it is replayed.

4 Jack in ditch

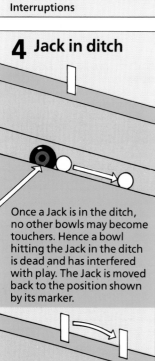

Once a Jack is in the ditch, no other bowls may become touchers. Hence a bowl hitting the Jack in the ditch is dead and has interfered with play. The Jack is moved back to the position shown by its marker.

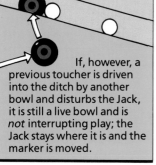

If, however, a previous toucher is driven into the ditch by another bowl and disturbs the Jack, it is still a live bowl and is *not* interrupting play; the Jack stays where it is and the marker is moved.

5 Dead Jack

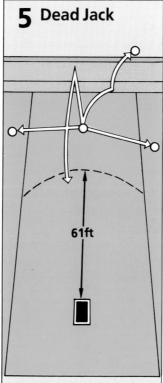

61ft

If the Jack is driven completely out of the side of the rink or over the bank or rebounds off the bank forward to a point within 61ft (66ft indoors) of the centre of the front of the mat, the Jack is dead and so the end also becomes dead. The end is replayed from the same direction.

6 Boundary Jack

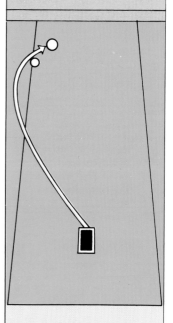

A Jack which has been knocked to the boundary line, but not completely outside it, is still live and bowls may be played onto it from outside the rink. If a bowl, however, (toucher or not) ends completely outside the rink it is dead and is removed to the bank.

7 Playing out of turn

If a player delivering a bowl plays out of turn, the bowl should be stopped by the opposing skip and played in its proper turn, but if it disturbs the Jack, a live bowl, or a toucher in the ditch then the opposing skip has two choices:

1   Leave it where it is.

2   Declare the end dead. The end is then replayed from the same direction, with the first player as before.

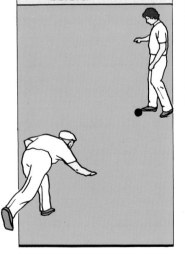

8 Omitting to play

If the result of an end has already been agreed upon, a player who has decided not to play a bowl cannot change his mind.

9 Damaged Jack

Should the Jack become damaged in play, the end is dead and is replayed from the same direction using a new Jack, with the first player as before.

10 Playing the wrong bowl

If you play one of your opponent's bowls by mistake, it is simply replaced by one of yours after it has come to rest.

11 Changing bowls

A player is not allowed to change the set of bowls used during a game, except when a bowl is sufficiently damaged to render it unplayable, or if a valid objection to the bowls being used is raised.

12 Bad light, rain

The end in progress is abandoned. The game is resumed later with scores as they were when the game stopped.

The Grip

There are two grips — the claw and the cradle.

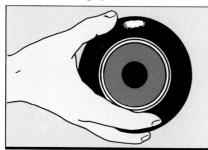 

The claw

The bowl is held in the fingers. The thumb is placed high and the fingers spread out underneath.

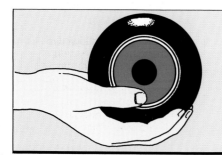 

The cradle

The bowl is cupped in the palm of the hand. The thumb is placed lower down.

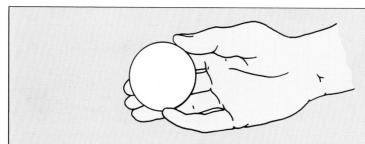

The Jack

The Jack is best played with a claw grip, well to the front of the fingers.

NOTE: In all grips keep the fingers under the bowl in the direction of aim.

Delivering a Bowl

Your delivery does not change whether you are bowling long or short. Adopt whatever stance comes naturally to you. It is, however, important to see that your feet are positioned correctly, i.e. orientated on the mat towards the line of play (see illustrations for forehand and backhand, below).

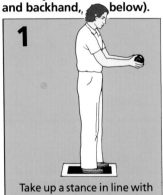

1

Take up a stance in line with the point of aim. Show the bowl its target. Left foot slightly forward, knees slightly bent.

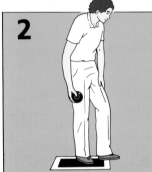

2

Swing back the bowling arm and the right shoulder. Bend left leg to keep balance. Left arm stays forward. It helps to maintain balance if your left hand rests on your left leg just above the knee.

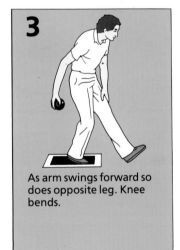

3

As arm swings forward so does opposite leg. Knee bends.

Forehand

The bowl is played off to the right. The shoulders are lined up in the direction of aim. The bias side of the bowl is next to the little finger.

Backhand

The bowl is played off to the left. Again the shoulders are lined up in the direction of aim. The bias is next to the thumb.

NOTE: The illustrations above are for a right-handed player; for a left-hander they would be reversed.

4

Foot completely forward. Arm swings foward in one smooth movement. Bowl released as it passes foot. Left hand still on your knee.

5

Follow through with your hand and arm along the delivery line as you release the bowl.

POINTS TO REMEMBER

● When you stand on the mat make sure you are facing the 'shoulder' of the hand you wish to play (see page 12).

● Use your body movement to propel the bowl – it is less tiring.

● Make sure you are gripping the bowl correctly but not too tightly.

● Develop a smooth swing.

● Follow through.

Foot fault

One foot must be *entirely* on, or above the mat at the moment of delivery – that is, when the bowl or Jack leaves the hand.

The player may lift the back foot during delivery providing it is clearly over the mat at the moment the bowl or Jack leaves the hand.

A bowl or Jack delivered with a foot fault may be declared dead.

The Basic Game

The object of the game is to get all your bowls closer to the Jack than your opponent's bowls.

The player with the closest bowl to the Jack wins the end, but the score depends on how many of your bowls are closer, and whether they are 'live bowls' or 'dead bowls' (see page 16). One shot is scored for each of your bowls that is closer to the Jack than any of your opponent's.

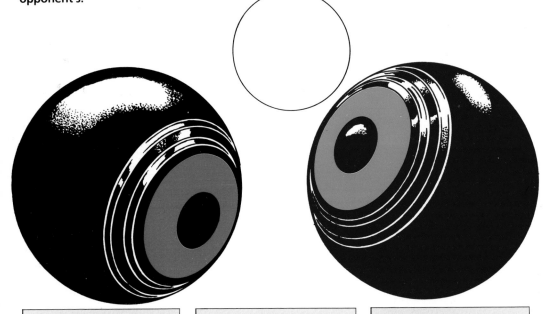

The toss

The players (or teams) toss to decide who plays first. The first player positions the mat, delivers the Jack, and plays the first bowl.

Order of play

The players deliver one bowl each alternately until all the bowls are played and the end is complete.

A new end

The next end is played from the opposite end of the rink. The winner of the previous end plays first. In other words – positions the mat, delivers the Jack, and plays the first bowl.

Scoring

The winner of an end is the player or team with the bowl closest to the Jack.

The number of shots scored, however, depends on how many of the winner's bowls are closer than the opposition's.

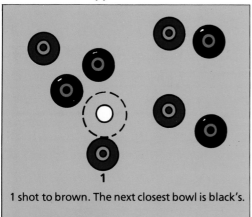

1 shot to brown. The next closest bowl is black's.

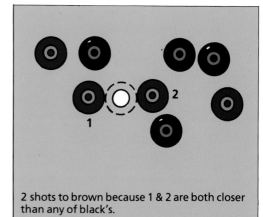

2 shots to brown because 1 & 2 are both closer than any of black's.

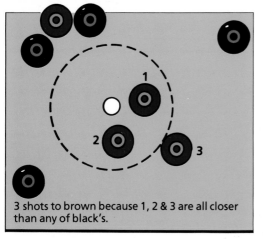

3 shots to brown because 1, 2 & 3 are all closer than any of black's.

4 shots to brown because all of brown's bowls are closer than any of black's.

Basic Shots

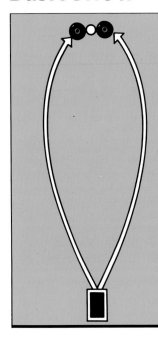

The draw

This is the most basic shot in bowls. Using a combination of weight and line, you 'draw' your bowl to a chosen point.

Your accuracy will depend on several factors:
1   **The bias and weight of your bowl.**
2   **The weight of your delivery.**
3   **The line you aim along.**
4   **The condition of the green. Long grass and wet ground slow the bowl, so it makes less length and the bias is less effective.**

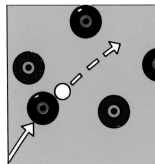

The trail shot

A trail shot is hard to play. The bowl comes up gently on the Jack, pushing it before the bowl. The two come to rest, still in contact, at the chosen point.

If the trail hits the Jack off-centre it will knock it to one side or the other. If it strikes the Jack too hard, the Jack will be knocked on ahead.

This shot is for an advanced player. You should have mastered the draw and practised the trail before considering its use. Also, the faster the green the more difficult the shot will become.

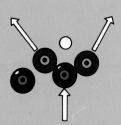

The firing shot

Also known as 'driving' or 'striking' this is a shot played so hard that it runs straight at the object bowl or the Jack.

Its aim is to break up a pattern in which your bowls are at a disadvantage, or in which you cannot get to the Jack. Sometimes if your opponent has three or four bowls in a scoring position, it is worth trying to run the Jack out of the rink and kill the end altogether.

It is a destructive shot with unpredictable results for inexperienced players. Not recommended for beginners.

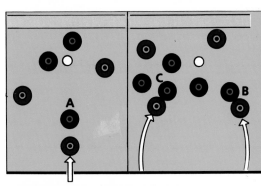

Guard shots

There are two guard shots, both of which are tactical ploys. The first is played directly in the line of the Jack (A) to prevent a firing shot by your opponent.

The second, played forehand (B) or backhand (C), is placed to prevent a trail shot from your opponent.

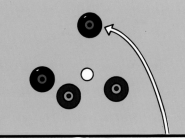

The best back

This is the deliberate placing of a bowl behind the Jack (but in front of the ditch). Its advantage is that should the Jack be knocked forward or into the ditch, then the back bowl is in a good scoring position.

An End

An end is the sequence of play from the positioning of the mat to the coming to rest of the last player's bowl.

To illustrate an end, here are eight shots which cover most of the basic possibilities. You are playing with the black bowls, and your opponent with the brown.

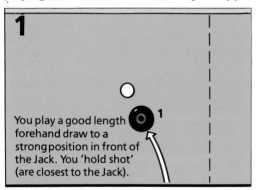

1 You play a good length forehand draw to a strong position in front of the Jack. You 'hold shot' (are closest to the Jack).

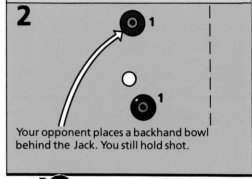

2 Your opponent places a backhand bowl behind the Jack. You still hold shot.

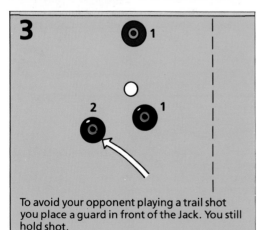

3 To avoid your opponent playing a trail shot you place a guard in front of the Jack. You still hold shot.

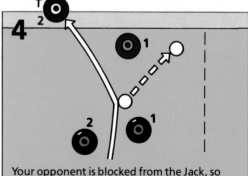

4 Your opponent is blocked from the Jack, so plays a firing shot which deflects the Jack to the corner, near the first bowl, and runs into the ditch. Because the bowl has touched the Jack, however, it remains a live bowl. Your opponent holds shot.

An End

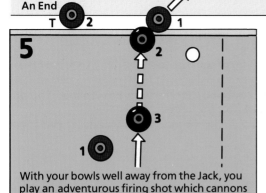

5

With your bowls well away from the Jack, you play an adventurous firing shot which cannons off your first bowl, driving it towards the ditch where it pushes your opponent's bowl over the edge.

Your opponent's bowl is removed as a dead bowl. You hold shot.

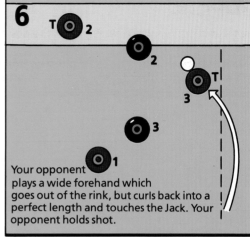

6

Your opponent plays a wide forehand which goes out of the rink, but curls back into a perfect length and touches the Jack. Your opponent holds shot.

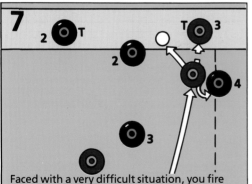

7

Faced with a very difficult situation, you fire into your opponent's bowl knocking it and the Jack into the ditch. Because your opponent's bowl was a toucher, both it and the Jack remain live in the ditch. Your bowl almost goes out, but just remains live. You hold shot.

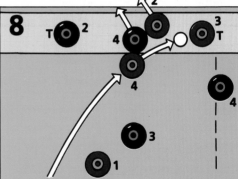

8

The Jack is in the ditch. Your opponent plays a fine wide backhand which goes into the ditch, taking your bowl with it and displacing the Jack. Neither is a toucher so both bowls are removed. The Jack is repositioned.

Your opponent wins the end by one shot.

NOTE: In the diagrams above, T = Toucher

Singles, Pairs, Triples and Fours

Singles

Two players (one on each side) play four bowls each. The first player positions the mat, delivers the Jack and plays the first bowl. The second player plays a bowl, then the first player a second bowl, and so on until all eight bowls are played. The maximum score for an end is four shots. The first player to 21 shots wins.

Pairs

Four players (two on each side) play four bowls each. The first players in each side play their four bowls alternately, as in singles, then the second players play their four bowls. The maximum score for an end is eight shots.

The game is played over 21 ends, or to a time limit. If the scores are equal at the end it is usual to play an extra end to find a winner.

Triples

Six players (three on each side) play three bowls each. The first players in the three sides play their three bowls in rotation. Then the second players in each side play their three bowls in rotation, and finally the third players (the skips) play their three bowls. The maximum score for an end is nine shots.

A triples game is played to 18 ends outdoors.

Fours

Eight players (four on each side) play two bowls each. The first players (the leads) in each of the four teams play their two bowls in rotation. Then the second players (the seconds), the third players (the thirds) and the fourth players (the skips) likewise. The maximum score for an end is eight shots.

A game is usually played to 21 ends or an agreed time.

Positions During Play

With up to eight players on a rink, it can get crowded. Regardless of how many players are involved, there are a few obvious courtesies to observe:

1	The player bowling is in possession of the rink.
2	Do not distract or obstruct your opponent.
3	Stand behind the bowler.
4	If you are at the 'head', stand beyond the Jack and to the side. Never stand directly behind it, or forward of it, or directly in front of it.

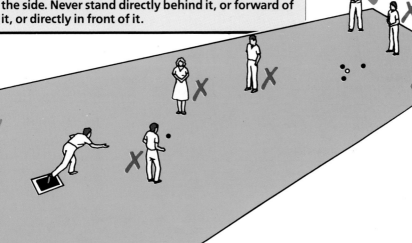

Practising

The basic shot in bowls is the draw. This is played both forehand and backhand and there are many variations. To become expert at the draw will take several years and so practice pays dividends.

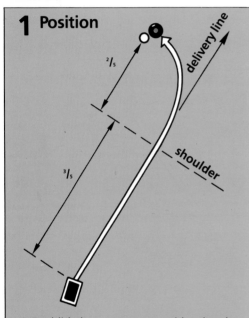

1 Position

1. Establish the exact spot you wish to bowl to finish.
2. Place the outside of your right foot on the delivery line.
3. Estimate the shoulder to be roughly ³/₅ along the line.
4. Practise this shot forehand and backhand.

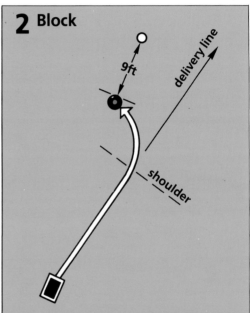

2 Block

A block shot is played to protect a good position you have developed around the Jack. To be effective it needs to be at least nine feet in from the Jack. You will need to fix your mind on this spot and aim for it, playing the bowl with less pace. Practise by delivering a bowl to the Jack and then playing a block. By this means you will learn the difference in pace and line required.

3 Trail

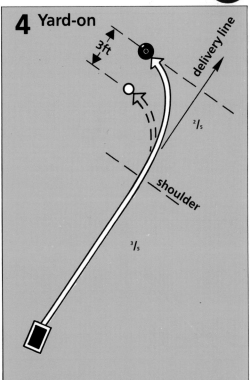

delivery line

²/₅

shoulder

³/₅

This is a difficult shot but one worth practising. Your aim is two-fold. You want to hit the Jack, which is a small target, but your delivery and pace are determined by the final position you want the bowl and Jack to occupy. Practise by bowling past the Jack to the correct length and then adjust till you can pick up the Jack on the way.

4 Yard-on

3ft

delivery line

²/₅

shoulder

³/₅

Yard-on is a useful shot because if the Jack is knocked back later in the game your bowl is likely to benefit.

It does not, however, want to be more than one yard behind the Jack and judging the weight of the bowl to get the extra yard of pace requires practice. Practise forehand and backhand.

Yard-on is also the term used to denote a shot used to push on to a bowl and stay in its place.

5 Wrest

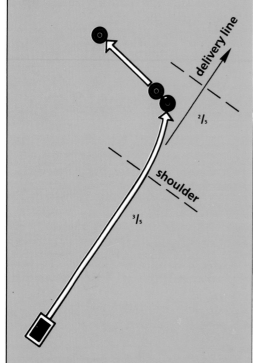

Your intention here is to replace one of your opponent's bowls with your own. Again you are aiming at an empty space beyond your opponent's bowl so your aim will be narrower.

Practise forehand and backhand till you learn the right amount of pace to punch your opponent's bowl aside but leave yours in position.

6 Wick

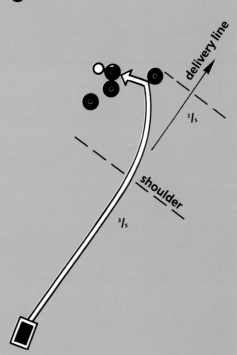

The wick is an extremely useful shot so why not practise it?

The object is to strike an opponent's bowl with a glancing shot to get your bowl into an otherwise unreachable position.

You must imagine the line your bowl must take to hit the opponent's bowl at the right point to get the required deflection. Line up some bowls and practise getting a deflection behind them.

Team Play

The basic rules and tactics are the same no matter how many players are involved, but the following points of etiquette should be observed during team games.

As an inexperienced player you will almost certainly play lead (first). Remember that this is a team effort, that the skip is in charge and that you must play as directed. Choose people you like and respect to play with and always play with that in mind.

1 Delivering the Jack

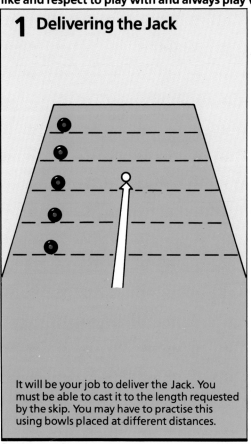

It will be your job to deliver the Jack. You must be able to cast it to the length requested by the skip. You may have to practise this using bowls placed at different distances.

2 Delivering the first bowl

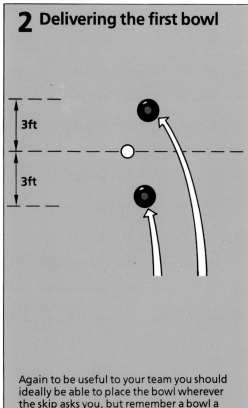

3ft

3ft

Again to be useful to your team you should ideally be able to place the bowl wherever the skip asks you, but remember a bowl a yard long is better than a bowl a yard short.

Flat Green Glossary

BACKHAND	Playing the bowl off to the left-hand side of the rink (right-handed player) so that the curve of the bowl is from left to right towards its objective. A left-handed backhand is played to the right-hand side of the rink.
BIAS	The degree to which a bowl will deviate from a straight path. This is determined by the shape of the bowl. There are official degrees of bias.
CENTRE LINE	An imaginary line that runs lengthwise down the centre of the rink.
DEAD BOWL	One which fails to travel 45 feet from the mat or comes to rest wholly outside the boundary of the rink or, being a non-toucher, ends in the ditch or rebounds from the bank.
DEAD END	An end which is considered not to have been played and so no score is recorded. The end is replayed.
DEAD JACK	A Jack which comes to rest wholly beyond the boundary of the rink or within 70 feet (75 feet indoors), in a straight line of play from the front of the mat. A rebounding Jack which comes to rest less than 61ft (66ft indoors) from the centre of the mat. If the Jack is dead, the end also becomes dead.
DELIVERY	The moment the bowl leaves the hand.
DRAW	The path a bowl will travel to reach its objective.
END	The sequence of play beginning with the placing of the mat and ending with the coming to rest of the last player's bowl.
FIRING	Also known as 'driving' or 'striking', this is a shot where a bowl is delivered at a very fast pace, usually with the intention of knocking the Jack or other bowls out of position.
FOREHAND	Playing the bowl off to the right-hand side of the rink (right-handed player) so that the curve of the bowl is from right to left of its objective. A left-handed forehand is played off to the left of the rink.
GUARD	A shot (also known as a 'Block') in which a bowl is deliberately placed to prevent the opponent playing a trail or firing shot.
HEAD	The Jack and all the bowls which have come to rest within the boundary.
JACK	The smaller white ball which is delivered first and at which the bowls are aimed. The Jack is without bias in Flat Green bowls.
LEADER	The first player.
LIVE BOWL	One that remains on the rink or a bowl in the ditch providing it has touched the Jack.
MEASURE	A device used to determine the distance between a bowl and the Jack.
SHOT	The bowl nearest the Jack.
SHOULDER	The point of the green where the bowl begins to curve inwards towards its objective.
SKIP	The last to bowl in pairs, triples and fours. The skip dictates the tactics of the game and is usually the most experienced player.
TOUCHER	A bowl which on its original course has touched the Jack, or falls over to touch the Jack before the next bowl is delivered. Touchers must be marked with chalk.
TRAIL	A bowl which rolls up to the Jack and moves it to another part of the rink.
TIED END	If the nearest bowls of both sides are <u>exactly</u> the same distance from, (or are both touching) the Jack, the end is tied and is recorded on the score card with a zero to each side.
WOOD	Another name for a bowl, a set of woods being a matching set of four bowls.

CROWN GREEN BOWLS

Crown Green bowls originated in the Lancashire area but has spread gradually to the surrounding counties and is growing in popularity. It is now played in an area from Cumbria to Warwickshire including Wales.

Unlike Flat Green bowls it is a game basically for two people although several games can be played on the green simultaneously.

The bowls used are the same but generally slightly smaller. The Jack and the mat, however, are different.

It is a skilful game, ideal for players of any age, constantly fascinating in its infinite variety.

The Green

The shape of the green may be square, oblong, or even round. There is usually a boundary ditch on all four sides.

The green takes its name from the raised central portion of the green called the crown. This varies in height and size, but can rise as much as eighteen inches higher than the edges.

The surface of the green is also not as level as in Flat Green, and may contain irregularities and peculiarities which will be more familiar to the local players than the visitor.

The green has an entrance which should be marked on one of the sides, from where play begins.

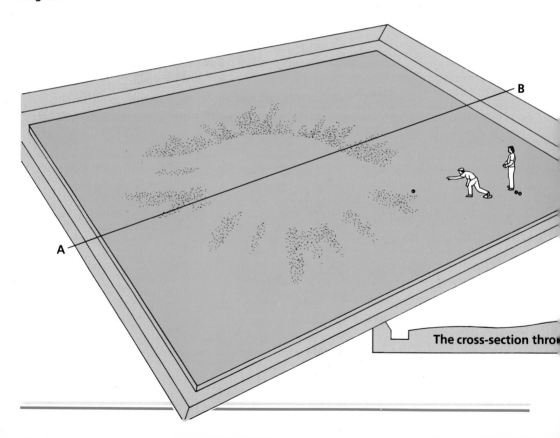

B

A

The cross-section thro▮

Equipment
Bowls

The bowls used in Crown Green are not the same as in Flat Green. Only two are used in a game and the only restriction is that a bowl should not weigh less than 2lbs, so players often carry several sets to suit the ground and the green.

In general lighter bowls are used than in Flat Green, and as the Jack has a standard bias (Bias 2) it is an advantage to use bowls with the same bias as the Jack.

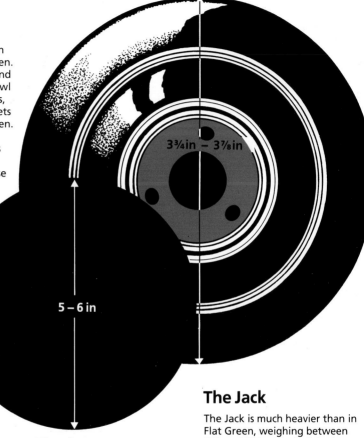

3¾in – 3⅞in

5 – 6 in

The Jack

The Jack is much heavier than in Flat Green, weighing between 653 and 680g. The Jack is also biased like a bowl and carries the British Crown Green Bowling Association (BCGBA) stamp showing a bias level 2.

It has a diameter of between 97 and 98.5mm.

The footer

The footer is the equivalent of the mat in Flat Green, usually of rubber, it is round and between 12.5 and 15cm in diameter.

Placing the Footer

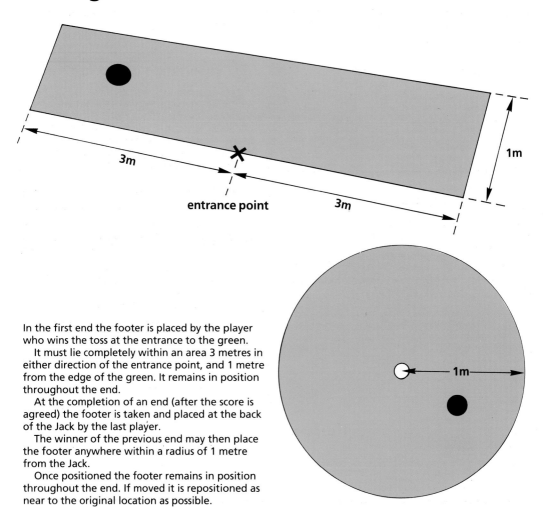

In the first end the footer is placed by the player who wins the toss at the entrance to the green.

It must lie completely within an area 3 metres in either direction of the entrance point, and 1 metre from the edge of the green. It remains in position throughout the end.

At the completion of an end (after the score is agreed) the footer is taken and placed at the back of the Jack by the last player.

The winner of the previous end may then place the footer anywhere within a radius of 1 metre from the Jack.

Once positioned the footer remains in position throughout the end. If moved it is repositioned as near to the original location as possible.

Setting a Mark

After positioning the footer at the entrance, the first player (called the leader) delivers the Jack anywhere on the green. This is called setting a Mark.
There are several restrictions:

1 Choose which hand

The hand with which the player delivers the Jack must play the bowls and all shots thereafter throughout the game. This is because an ambidextrous player would benefit from changing hands on certain slopes.

2 Hand and foot

If the right hand delivers the Jack, then the right toe must be on the footer at the moment of delivering the Jack or the bowls. If the player uses the left hand, then the left toe must touch the footer at the moment of delivery.

3 Distance

If the Jack does not travel at least 19 metres from the centre of the footer or goes off the green, it is redelivered by the other player and so on until the Mark is set. The leader, however, still plays the first bowl.

4 Opponent's objection

If the opponent feels a Mark is not legitimate, it may only be questioned after the leader has played the first bowl. This is because there is an advantage in setting the Mark – the leader will follow the Jack with the same line and weight for the bowl. To interrupt this advantage to measure the Mark would be unfair if the Mark proved subsequently to be good.

5 Leader's objection

There is no such advantage when the second player sets the Mark (due to a failed Mark from the leader) because the first bowl is always played by the leader.

6 Bias

The Jack can be played with the bias on the little finger (forehand), or the bias on the thumb (backhand). The opponent must be able to observe which is to be played.

Dead Bowls

A bowl may hit the Jack or other bowls, but for a bowl to count in the scoring it must be live at the completion of the end.

A BOWL IS DEAD:

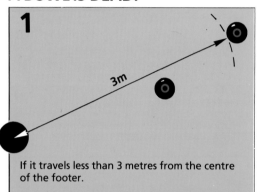

1

If it travels less than 3 metres from the centre of the footer.

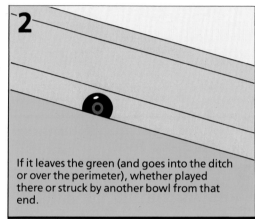

2

If it leaves the green (and goes into the ditch or over the perimeter), whether played there or struck by another bowl from that end.

3

If the player drops or misdelivers the bowl and cannot recover it without taking his foot off the footer.

4

If one of the other player's bowls is delivered by mistake. In this case the bowl is returned to the opponent, and one of the offender's bowls is forfeited.

Interruptions

There are often several games going on simultaneously, criss-crossing the green, so collisions are a little more common than in Flat Green bowls.

BEFORE THE MARK IS SET

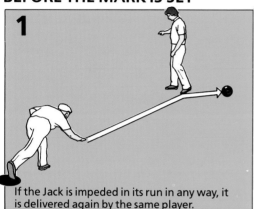

1 If the Jack is impeded in its run in any way, it is delivered again by the same player.

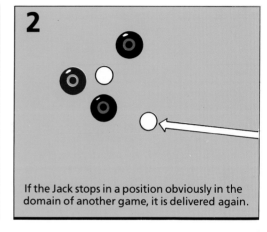

2 If the Jack stops in a position obviously in the domain of another game, it is delivered again.

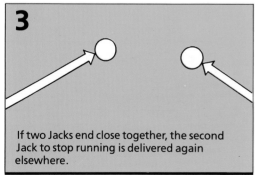

3 If two Jacks end close together, the second Jack to stop running is delivered again elsewhere.

NOTE: If a Jack or bowl is obviously going to impede another game, it should be stopped and returned to be replayed.

AFTER A MARK IS SET

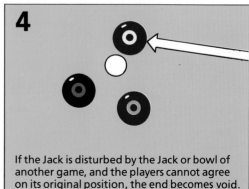

4 If the Jack is disturbed by the Jack or bowl of another game, and the players cannot agree on its original position, the end becomes void.

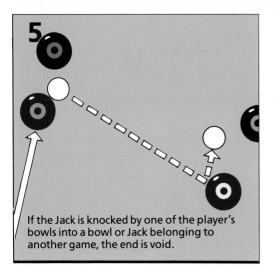

If the Jack is knocked by one of the player's bowls into a bowl or Jack belonging to another game, the end is void.

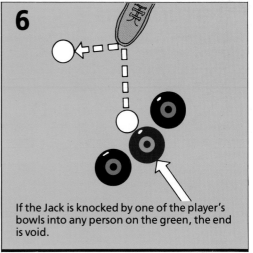

If the Jack is knocked by one of the player's bowls into any person on the green, the end is void.

If the Jack is disturbed by a person or other outside cause whilst stationary, it should be replaced in the original position unless the players are unable to agree, in which case the end is void.

JACK OFF THE GREEN

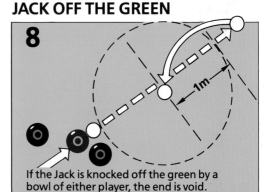

If the Jack is knocked off the green by a bowl of either player, the end is void.

The Jack is replaced 1 metre from the edge of the green, and whoever made the previous Mark makes it again, placing the footer anywhere within a 1-metre radius around the Jack.

MOVING BOWLS

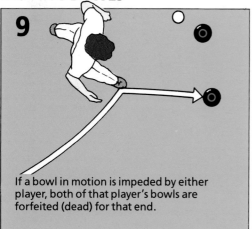

9

If a bowl in motion is impeded by either player, both of that player's bowls are forfeited (dead) for that end.

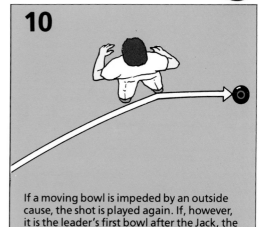

10

If a moving bowl is impeded by an outside cause, the shot is played again. If, however, it is the leader's first bowl after the Jack, the leader may also reset the Mark if desired.

STILL BOWLS

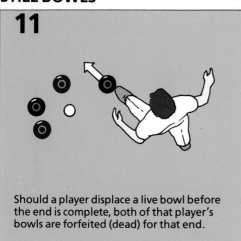

11

Should a player displace a live bowl before the end is complete, both of that player's bowls are forfeited (dead) for that end.

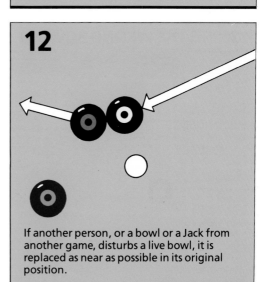

12

If another person, or a bowl or a Jack from another game, disturbs a live bowl, it is replaced as near as possible in its original position.

FOLLOWING BOWLS

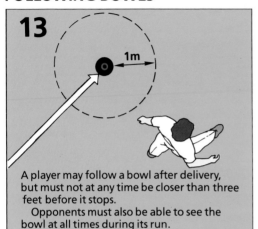

13

1m

A player may follow a bowl after delivery, but must not at any time be closer than three feet before it stops.
  Opponents must also be able to see the bowl at all times during its run.

14

If a player attempts to speed up or slow down a bowl during its run, that bowl is dead. If the player offends twice in this way the game is awarded to the opponent, but the offender's score stands.

PLAYING THE WRONG BOWL

15

If a player uses an opponent's bowl, it is returned to the opponent and the offender loses one of his bowls as a penalty.

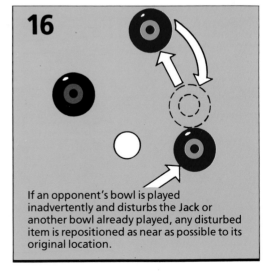

16

If an opponent's bowl is played inadvertently and disturbs the Jack or another bowl already played, any disturbed item is repositioned as near as possible to its original location.

Straight Peg/Round Peg

The most intriguing aspect of Crown Green bowls is that the slope of the green affects the bowl as much as the bias.

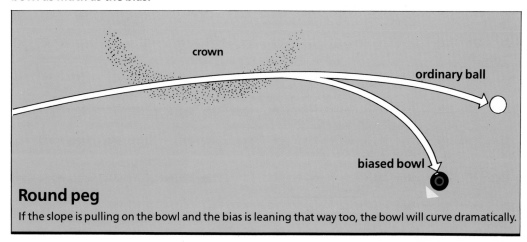

crown

ordinary ball

biased bowl

Round peg

If the slope is pulling on the bowl and the bias is leaning that way too, the bowl will curve dramatically.

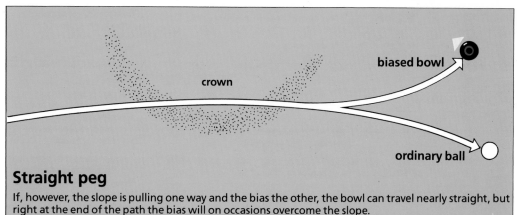

biased bowl

crown

ordinary ball

Straight peg

If, however, the slope is pulling one way and the bias the other, the bowl can travel nearly straight, but right at the end of the path the bias will on occasions overcome the slope.

Crown Green Glossary

BIAS The degree to which a bowl will deviate from a straight path. This is determined by the shape of the bowl. There are official degrees of bias.

BLOCK Another name for the Jack.

BOBBY A shot (also known as a 'guard' or 'block') in which a bowl is deliberately placed to prevent the opponent playing a trail or firing shot.

CLAW GRIP A method of holding the bowl with the thumb high up on the bowl and the fingers spread.

CRADLE GRIP A method of holding the bowl with the palm cupped.

DEAD BOWL One which fails to travel 3 metres from the centre of the footer, goes off the green, or ends in the ditch.

DEAD END A void end for which no score is recorded. The end is replayed.

DEAD WOOD A bowl that cannot score because of rule breaking.

DELIVERY The moment the bowl leaves the hand.

DITCH The depression usually surrounding the green which marks the boundary of the playing surface. Also known as the 'gutter'.

END The sequence of play beginning with the placing of the footer and ending with the coming to rest of the last player's bowl.

FIRING Also known as 'driving' or 'striking', this is a shot where a bowl is delivered at a very fast pace, usually with the intention of knocking the Jack or other bowls out of position.

FOOTER The equivalent of the mat in Flat Green bowls.

HEAD The Jack and all the bowls which have come to rest within the boundary.

JACK The small white, black or yellow ball which is delivered first and at which the bowls are aimed. The Jack has a full No. 2 Bias in Crown Green bowls.

JACK HEADER A bowl that finishes in front and touches the Jack.

LEADER The first player.

MARK Correctly delivering the Jack in Crown Green bowls is known as 'setting the Mark'.

MEASURE A device used to determine the distance between a bowl and the Jack.

PEG Round peg is where the Jack and bowls are bowled with the bias facing away from the crown; straight peg is a Jack or bowl delivered with the bias facing the crown.

SHOT The bowl nearest the Jack.

TIED END If the nearest bowls of both sides are exactly the same distance from, or are both touching, the Jack, the end is tied and is recorded on the score card as no end.

WOOD Another name for a bowl, a set of woods in Crown Green being a matching set of two bowls.